THE STORY *of* GRACE DARLING

CONTENTS

Written by Maureen Haselhurst
Photographs by Brian Wade

Collins Educational
An imprint of HarperCollins*Publishers*

Great Britain

The Shetland Isles

Inverness
Aberdeen

North Sea

North Atlantic
Ocean

Edinburgh
Glasgow

Farne Islands

Newcastle upon Tyne

Belfast

Leeds

Irish Sea

Dublin
Manchester

Birmingham

London

Cardiff

Southampton

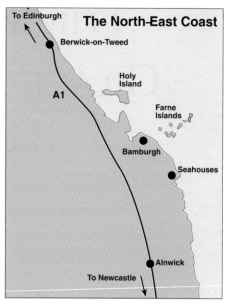

The North-East Coast

To Edinburgh

Berwick-on-Tweed

Holy
Island

A1

Farne
Islands

Bamburgh

Seahouses

Alnwick

To Newcastle

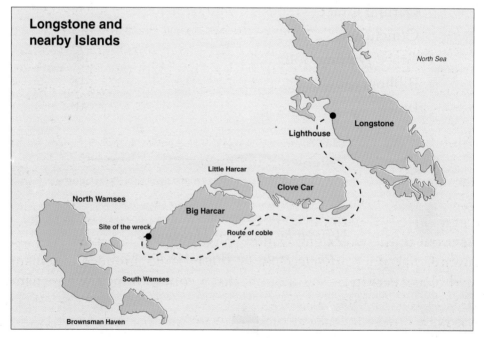

Longstone and nearby Islands

North Sea

Longstone

Lighthouse

Little Harcar

Clove Car

North Wamses

Big Harcar

Site of the wreck

Route of coble

South Wamses

Brownsman Haven

Introduction

In the grim dawn of a storm-tossed morning, a young woman was on watch high in a lighthouse tower. A short distance away, pounded by savage waves, a ship lay wrecked on the perilous rocks. In the next few hours the unknown young woman was to take her place in history by her involvement in an extremely hazardous rescue. The year was 1838 and the young woman was Grace Darling.

Had it happened today, her story would be made into a television documentary, for it has all the ingredients of a sensational drama. Had it happened today, we may not have been too surprised that a woman was central to the story. At that time, however, the idea that a woman would have the strength and nerve to rescue people from a shipwreck was quite astonishing.

Grace Darling's fascinating story is set against the isolated background of the windswept Farne Islands in Northumberland. It has gone through many changes. Artists altered her image and painted her in different ways in their pictures. Newspapers and even children's comics meddled with the basic facts. Some stories claimed that she went out to the wreck alone and implied that her father was a coward. The story of Grace Darling has become shrouded in romantic mythology. Perhaps it was thought that a young woman, whose name was so perfectly suited to a hero, may not prove quite so attractive if it was known that she had set out on her mission of mercy with her hair in curling rags!

The aim of this book is to tell the events of Grace Darling's life as accurately as possible. Two books have provided the major sources of information. The first of these is *The Journal of William Darling 1795-1860*. This is written in the style of a ship captain's log, in which Grace Darling's father recorded weather conditions, wrecks, sea rescues, visitors, living conditions and important family events during his years as a lighthouse keeper. The journal was edited by his daughter, Thomasin Darling, Grace's elder sister, who was also the co-author of *Grace Darling: Her True Story*, along with Daniel Atkinson. The second book is *Grace Darling and Her Times*, written in 1932 by Constance Smedley. Because of her in-depth research, she is acknowledged by local historians as being a reliable authority on Grace and her life. Reference has also been made to various letters that Grace wrote or received during her life which are on display at the Grace Darling Museum. These sources have helped to disentangle the fact from the fantasy that has made a myth of the Grace Darling story.

The Darling Family Tree

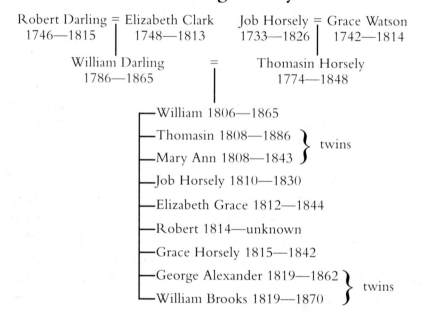

Robert Darling = Elizabeth Clark
1746—1815   1748—1813

Job Horsely = Grace Watson
1733—1826   1742—1814

William Darling   =   Thomasin Horsely
1786—1865   1774—1848

- William 1806—1865
- Thomasin 1808—1886 } twins
- Mary Ann 1808—1843 }
- Job Horsely 1810—1830
- Elizabeth Grace 1812—1844
- Robert 1814—unknown
- Grace Horsely 1815—1842
- George Alexander 1819—1862 } twins
- William Brooks 1819—1870 }

The Darlings

It was December 1815 when, at three weeks old, Grace Horsely Darling made her first trip across to Brownsman Island. She had been born on 24 November in her grandfather's house in the fishing village of Bamburgh. The Darling family was already a large one, Grace being the seventh child. Her father, William Darling, was the lighthouse keeper on Brownsman, but, unlike the isolated lives of later keepers, he was allowed to have his wife and children with him. Consequently, the island became their family home.

It is impossible to write about the Darlings without also writing about their environment. Their lives were greatly influenced by the desolate Farne Islands on which they lived and by the people and culture of the fishing villages along the coast. However, the greatest factor in their lives, indeed what dictated their whole existence, was the sea.

This stretch of isolated Northumbrian coast is wild and exceptionally beautiful. It is a place where miles of sand dunes, spiked with sharp grasses, run down to beaches where pale yellow ribbons of fine sand stretch out. It is a place where sinister cliffs rise grimly from dark coves. Off the coast lie the wreck-strewn reefs of the Farne Islands. There are twenty-eight islands in all: some are just flat slabs of rock, only visible when the tide ebbs, while others rear high out of the sea and are topped by lighthouse towers. The air is full of spindrift – the spray blown up from the surface of the sea – and the wings of thousands of screaming, swooping sea birds. Above all, there is the never-ending sound of the sea.

An aerial view of the Farne Islands

The tiny coastal village of Bamburgh hasn't changed greatly since Grace Darling's time. It is a compact collection of neat, grey-stoned cottages, set around a copse of tall trees. A memorial to Grace faces out to sea from the quiet graveyard of the church of St Aidan where she is buried, and the relics of her life can be seen in the simple building that houses the Grace Darling Museum.

Above the village looms Bamburgh Castle, with its massive red stone ramparts rising dramatically from a lofty crag. To the east the castle faces out beyond the wide dunes across the North Sea, while to the west its towering walls shelter the village far below. In Grace Darling's time, Bamburgh Castle was run by a committee of clergymen called the Crewe Trustees. Their aim was to improve the quality of life in the village. The area was isolated. Cut off from the benefits offered by town life, such as schools, hospitals and shops, life in Bamburgh and the other tiny coastal villages was often harsh. Many of the families earned their living from fishing which gave them a low income.

Bamburgh Castle as seen from the village of Bamburgh

The Crewe Trustees put the castle to good use and provided many of the missing facilities, largely free of charge. Inside the castle there was a hospital, a hostel for shipwrecked sailors and a Free Shop where the Trustees sold basic food without making a profit, allowing the poorer families to afford a more wholesome diet. The castle also had a free public lending library where William Darling, an avid reader, could often be found. Part of the castle had been converted into a boys' school where the standards were high and where Grace's brothers went for a time. There is some confusion over whether Grace herself ever went to school. Certainly her father was responsible for most of her education. As an adult she wrote in a letter:

> *I have been brought up on the islands, learned to read and write by my parents... Our books are principally Divinity... Geography, History, Voyages and Travels, with Maps, so that Father can show us any part of the World, and give us a description of the people, manners and customs, so it is our own blame if we be ignorant of either what is done, or what ought to be done.* [1]

Life on Brownsman Island was demanding but gave the Darling children a free and remarkably happy childhood. Their grandfather had been the first lighthouse keeper there and his position was inherited by their father William Darling. When he married, his wife, Thomasin, was thirty-one and he just nineteen. Nine children followed in rapid succession. Being a lighthouse keeper, William Darling was well-respected locally, and in newspaper reports after the famous rescue, he was described as "wise" and "venerable". Thomasin Darling's life isn't so well documented, but there is the impression that she was a busy, homely woman, always spinning, washing and sewing, and expecting her daughters to do the same.

The family's home on Brownsman Island was a small cottage, close to the lighthouse tower, which rose thirteen metres above the rock. With two adults, nine growing children and Happy, the Newfoundland dog, the cottage must have been rather crowded. The island was treeless, but rabbits thrived amongst the coarse grass and the family were able to keep a few sheep and goats. They had a small walled garden sheltered from the worst of the winds and here they grew vegetables and flowers. Mr Darling recorded the frustrations of keeping such an exposed

1 Letter dated 25 January, 1839, sent to Miss S Price of Nottingham

garden in his *Journal*. Several times over the years that they lived on Brownsman, storms and high tides swept it away:

> *Two tremendous gales… in the garden small seedlings being all above ground were totally blown off or destroyed.* [2]

Mr Darling was an excellent shot and brought home rabbits, wild duck, teal and widgeon to eat. Fish was also a large part of their diet: Mr Darling caught cod, herring and haddock which were then preserved in salt, in readiness for bad weather conditions which often made it impossible to go out of doors for food. Thus, with fresh meat, fish, vegetables and hard-boiled sea gulls' eggs, which apparently taste fishy, the Darlings enjoyed a balanced diet. Drinking water and other necessities were brought over from Bamburgh by boat.

The cottage and ruined lighthouse on Brownsman Island

2 *The Journal of William Darling 1795-1860.* Dated 26 and 27 April, 1813

The family was relatively well off for the time. Mr Darling's salary was £70 per year plus salvage, which was a payment for anything of value pulled from the sea, normally after a shipwreck. If people were rescued, he earned another fee of £1 per person, which was called a bounty. The family's living accommodation was free and their food cost them next to nothing. However, it must be remembered that Mrs Darling and the children worked as unpaid labour, each taking their turn at keeping watch and shouldering the drudgery of cleaning the lighthouse. They topped up their income during the summer months by running a sort of early Victorian Bed and Breakfast for birdwatchers – a hobby that was just coming into fashion. Mr Darling was an authority on sea birds and Grace had a large collection of their eggs. Mr Darling often shot specimens of the birds to send to the Newcastle museum. While this would be totally unacceptable now, at that time there was a growing interest in wildlife and the question of conservation didn't arise.

The Darling children had a healthy life. They were always in the fresh air and had plenty of exercise climbing the many stairs to the lantern chamber. In those days when many babies died, there is no mention of any of the children even being ill. They were completely at home on the sea and learnt how to handle a boat at a very early age. The family boat was a traditional Northumbrian coble, a large, sturdy rowing boat used for fishing, that needed three people at the oars. The Darling's coble would have been in the family for years and was the same one used by Grace for her famous rescue.

From the age of eight or nine, the boys were expected to put to sea with their father to pick up salvage and even to pull survivors from the water. Mr Darling's knowledge of sailing and the seas around his islands was exceptional. He taught his children well and, remarkably, none of them were ever hurt. The ability to handle a boat became even more essential when a new lighthouse was built on one of the

The coble *Grace Darling*

Outer Farnes. Mr Darling was promoted to the position of First
Keeper. The family's new home was to be a tower, twenty-five
metres high. It was the Longstone Lighthouse which was to
become infamous.

The Longstone

Though there had been beacons burning on the Farnes for a thousand years, the islands had become the graveyard for countless ships. For many years, Mr Darling had felt that a new and much higher light should be erected on Longstone. The greater the distance that the warning light could be built out into the open sea, the safer it would be for passing ships to steer away from the threat of the most dangerous of the rocks, and Longstone was by far the best site. However, building a structure that could withstand the severe North Sea conditions on a stretch of rock that was often submerged was obviously going to be difficult. Despite the structural problems, in 1825 the lighthouse authority, Trinity House, funded the construction of the Longstone Light. Over the course of that year, a circular tower constructed from massive granite blocks began to rise from the island. Building it proved to be a challenge for the engineers. The bleak, deserted island was invaded by a gang of labourers and masons who lived in a stone shed they built for themselves and nicknamed 'the barracks'. Despite all the difficulties, the tower was completed before Christmas and on 15 February, 1826, a new and brighter light shone out across the sea.

Grace was ten when the Darlings moved across from Brownsman Island to the even more remote Longstone. It was little more than a slab of rock about two metres above sea level where nothing would grow. Almost every day, the family had to row across to Brownsman to gather fresh vegetables from their garden and feed the livestock. On Longstone, their home was the tower itself. Despite its massive walls, it would sway and shudder in storm conditions under the force of the wind and sea, and occasionally, waves would actually sweep over the top of the tower. The Longstone's looming walls were painted red on the outside to make it more visible against the grey northern skies.

The Longstone Lighthouse during construction – the 'barracks' can be seen to the right of the picture

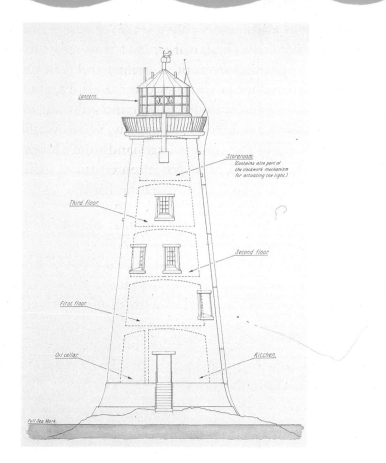

The original cross-section plan of the Longstone Lighthouse

All the rooms were circular, rising from a large living room/kitchen on the ground floor, going up the winding staircase, past bedrooms of decreasing diameter to the very top where the lantern chamber was. This housed the oil lamp with its revolving reflectors of silvered copper mounted on an iron frame. Here in the glass-walled lantern chamber, the noise of the elements was often tremendous. William Darling's journal makes frequent references to the glass in the lantern being broken by large birds thrown against it by the wind:

A curlew broke one square glass in the Lantern, falling dead. [3]

3 *The Journal of William Darling 1795-1860.* Dated 25 October, 1825

The oil lamp had to be constantly topped up and cleaned. The reflectors and the glass of the lantern had to be polished frequently in order to make sure the light kept its brilliance. Cleaning the outside of the lantern chamber was perhaps the most hazardous duty that the Darlings had to perform. A narrow balcony ran around the outer circumference of the lantern and a narrow, vertical ladder led to the very top. From here, with only metal handholds to grab, the glass had to be cleaned. In the winter, it was often encrusted with snow that froze onto the surface and obliterated the light.

The Longstone Light shone about eighteen kilometres out to sea and flashed a white beam every twenty seconds. It revolved on a platform driven by a clockwork winding gear which needed to be wound by hand, rather like a gigantic grandfather clock. Huge weights, like pendulums, hung down a metal tube to the foot of the tower. If these weights ever jammed, the winding gear in the lantern tower had to be turned by hand. The keeper's responsibility was never to allow the light to go out and the greatest offence a keeper could commit was to fall asleep while on watch.

The Longstone Lighthouse today

Today, what used to be the living room of the Longstone Lighthouse is filled with up-to-date technology that makes it possible for the light to operate without a lighthouse keeper. The door to the tower is now locked and the Longstone is deserted once again. In Grace's time, however, it was cosily furnished with solid armchairs, a sofa and a grandfather clock. A kettle simmered over the fire that always blazed in the iron grate and heated the cooking range. Stuffed sea birds were displayed in every nook and cranny and the mantelpieces were cluttered with tea caddies and salt boxes. Grace's room was the smallest and the highest, underneath the lantern chamber. It was just

Grace's bedroom. The metal tube to the left of the picture runs centrally down the whole height of the lighthouse and contains the weights that hang from the winding gear. The plaque on the wall commemorates the rescue.

over three metres in diameter, with white painted walls and a small rectangular window looking out over the restless sea.

The Longstone was the place where the Darling children grew up. There were new duties to be done and someone constantly on watch both by night and day, every day of the year. Mr Darling's employers were Trinity House, the authority in charge of most of the lighthouses in the United Kingdom. They expected a high standard of loyalty and discipline from their employees and encouraged them to see themselves as public servants with responsibility for the safety of ships and sailors. The Lighthouse Regulations stated that they were to keep detailed records of weather, tides and shipping and were to keep the lighthouse ship-shape and clean. The Darlings had always to be in a fit condition to receive a visit from a member of Trinity House, who could drop in on them without any prior warning. There were even strict rules about personal hygiene and behaviour. Trinity House Regulations expected them to be:

Cleanly in themselves and linen and orderly in their families.

Between lighthouse duties, Mr Darling held school lessons in the lantern chamber, taught his children local folk songs and accompanied them on his fiddle. He was a religious man, but also kind and fun-loving. However, he strongly disapproved of novels, which he banned, saying they were a pure waste of time. Poor Grace may well have thought that she was missing out, as she wrote in a letter shortly after the rescue:

Romances, novels and plays are books my father will not allow a place for in our house, for he says they are throwing away time. [4]

Time passed and one by one the Darling children left the island to make their own way in life. The older boys worked on the mainland while Grace's sisters also moved away. Grace, however, stayed on Longstone. With fewer hands to do the work, life must have been hard for her and she may well have felt lonely. However, the family

4 Letter dated 25 January, 1839, sent to Miss S Price of Nottingham

Thomasin Darling
Late Longstone Light June 31st 1846

William Darling in later life

A portrait of Thomasin Darling
painted by M Laidler in 1846

always got back together at Christmas and in 1834, when Grace was twenty, they all gathered at the lighthouse again for the festive season.

It was therefore coincidental that the boys were on Longstone when a particularly nasty storm blew up and a coal boat named *Autumn* was wrecked on the hazardous Knavestone. Mr Darling's journal briefly records their rescue of the sole survivor, a James Logan.

He wrote:

Wind S. by E. fresh gale. 11 p.m. The sloop Autumn... *struck east point of Knivestone*[*] *and immediately sank. Crew of three men; two lost, one saved by the light-keeper, and three sons, viz. [namely] William, Robert and George, after a struggle of three hours. Having lost two oars on the rock, had a very narrow escape.* [5]

The extract from William Darling's journal

This was the only reference Mr Darling ever made to the danger faced either by himself or his family.

George, the youngest of the brothers, wrote a longer account of what happened. He noted that at eight o'clock on the morning of 28 December, Grace was keeping watch in the lantern chamber and spotted a man clinging to the Knavestone rock. Within minutes, Mr Darling and the three brothers had launched the coble. There was a

*now called Knavestone
5 *The Journal of William Darling 1795-1860.* Dated 27 December, 1834

high-flowing tide and a strong gale blowing and it was impossible to attempt a landing on the rock where the shipwrecked man, Logan, was, in Mr Darling's words, becoming "frantic". These were the days before life jackets or life buoys and they tried to float a spar of wood to him with a rope attached, but it was useless. They took the coble dangerously near the rocks where Logan was by now up to his armpits in water. He managed to throw himself into the boat while the Darlings fended it off the rocks with their oars. Then disaster struck, as two of the oars broke. Robert and George plunged over the side and, swimming through the heavy swell, they somehow managed to push the boat in front of them and get it away from the Knavestone. George wrote:

> Robert and George, the only two who could swim, had to quit the boat and help her off the rock. It was, even for them, imminent risk in such a sea, but they did it. It was a miracle that the boat was not destroyed, when all five must have perished. [6]

It may seem surprising that not all of them could swim, but at that time many sailors harboured the superstition that the ability to swim brought bad luck.

Using their one remaining oar and a small amount of sail, the rescuers battled through the heavy seas until they eventually got back to Longstone. It was hours before the traumatised Logan was able to talk about how the rest of his crew mates had drowned. It seems that the Master of *Autumn* had been wearing his long sea boots which had filled with water and dragged him down.

Courageous as this rescue may have been, it was not widely reported; indeed if it wasn't for George's account, we should know nothing more than the short note in his father's journal. However, the next major rescue undertaken by the Darling family was to change all their lives.

6 George's account included by Thomasin Darling in *The Journal of William Darling 1795-1860*

George Darling who was involved in the
Autumn rescue, with his twin William Brooks

The Wreck

It was some time before dawn on the morning of 7 September, 1838, and Mr Darling had been on watch all night in the lantern chamber. He had become alarmed by the ferocity of an autumn storm that had blown up overnight. The air was filled with a fury of spume and spray that dashed against the lantern windows. The lighthouse was engulfed in a heaving seascape of rollers that smashed onto the tiny island in a turmoil of wild water. It was one of the worst storms that Mr Darling could remember.

William Darling was worried that the family's coble would break away from its mooring. He had already tried to secure it, but the force of the sea was too strong for him. Grace's younger brother, William Brooks, would normally have been there to help; but he was on the mainland helping with the herring catch in Seahouses and couldn't get back to Longstone because of the storm. Consequently, it was Grace who helped to secure the boat that storm-tossed morning. So began the chain of events that, within the next few hours, would transform her from an unknown, twenty-two year old lighthouse keeper's daughter into a national hero.

Being at the top of the tower, Grace's bedroom window would be above all but the highest waves. It was a quarter to five when she happened to look out in the grey dawn and saw that a dark shape was

The view from Grace's bedroom window across to Harcar Rocks. Clove Car is in the foreground and Big Harcar in the background.

rearing out of the waves. A ship had impaled itself on the black teeth of the Harcar Rocks.

The ship that was breaking itself against Big Harcar was the *Forfarshire*. It was one of the new breed of steamships that were gradually to take over from sail and ran regularly from Hull up the north-east coast to Dundee, carrying both cargo and passengers. It was a luxury vessel, one of the first to have passenger cabins and a dining room. On this last and tragic voyage, the *Forfarshire* had left Hull at midnight on 5 September, 1838. Mr Darling's journal records that it was carrying cargo and about sixty passengers and crew. One of the passengers was

The sailing timetable of the *Forfarshire*

the wife of the ship's captain, Captain Humble. Sadly, neither of them survived.

Shortly after leaving Hull, the weather began to worsen and, to add to the problems, the engineer reported that the boilers had sprung a leak. No-one is sure why Captain Humble didn't return to port as the storm blew up and the leak in the boilers worsened. Down in the engine room the crew was floundering in boiling water.

As night closed in, the ship fought its way up the coast. The tragic chain of events started when, off the coast of St Abbs Head, north of Berwick-on-Tweed, the engines failed and the ship began to drift back southwards. The paddle wheel was now powerless to steer the ship because of the engine failure. The crew hoisted the sails, but the combination of the gale and the weight of the huge wheel dragged the ship off course. In their cabins below, most of the passengers slept, unaware of the danger.

Some of the crew began to panic and eight of them launched a lifeboat. They escaped over the side with one of the passengers.

Somehow they managed to stay afloat and were picked up by a sloop the following day off the coast of Tynemouth. It seems unjust that many of the loyal crew, who stayed with the crippled ship, drowned when it went down.

As the *Forfarshire* was driven south, a light was spotted on the landward side. Captain Humble took it to be the light of the Inner Farne Lighthouse and used what little steerage he had to guide the ship towards what he thought were more sheltered waters. However, the Captain was mistaken. What he had seen was the light on Longstone that warned ships away from the lethal rocks. The ship drifted relentlessly towards its fate and, at about four o'clock in the morning, it was thrown against Big Harcar. Within fifteen minutes, it had broken in half as if it had been little more than a piece of driftwood. Forty-three passengers and crew went down with the ship as the stern section sank, leaving the forward section, the bows, steeply angled on the tusk of Big Harcar.

While this was happening, Thomasin Darling was on watch. Although the family kept the wreck under constant surveillance through their telescope, the poor light and the height of the waves made it impossible to see whether there were any survivors. It wasn't until seven o'clock that they spotted a group of people clinging to the rocks.

William Darling wrote in his journal:

> *One quarter before five, my daughter observed a vessel on the Harker*, but owing to the darkness and spray going over her, could not observe any person on the wreck, although the glass was incessantly applied until near seven o'clock.* [7]

Reports of the wreck of the *Forfarshire* were relatively consistent up to this part of the incident, but from this point on, accounts of what occurred varied widely. Events appear to have been dramatised and it

---

* now called Harcar rock

7 *The Journal of William Darling 1795-1860.* Dated 7 September, 1838

is difficult to know exactly what happened. For example, the words of a popular folk song later written about Grace run like this:

'Help! Help!' She could hear the cry of the shipwreck'd crew… [8]

It would have been impossible to hear anything above the howl of the raging wind and water. Of course it's a minor detail and was probably an example of dramatic licence, when a writer exaggerates the truth to make his or her writing more powerful, but nevertheless it shows how the story began to be told inaccurately. People wrote what they wanted to believe, or maybe what they guessed had happened, and the facts became clouded. However, what is indisputable is that there were indeed, survivors clinging to the Harcar Rocks and rescuing them in such a violent storm would be a challenge, which even our emergency rescue services today would find hazardous. It seems incredible that the Darlings with their basic resources should even consider it.

Reports of Mr Darling's initial reaction on hearing of the shipwreck differ. The local folk song suggests that he thought that rescue was out of the question with the sea as it was. The song continues:

Tis madness to face that raging sea!

The implication is that Mr Darling was rather cowardly and had to be pressed into the rescue by his pleading daughter. However, William Darling was a seasoned life-saver and had proved his courage time and time again. Grace's elder sister, Thomasin Darling, attempted to put the record straight:

It is very likely that the proposal to aid her father in the boat first came from Grace; but had he not himself thought the attempt practicable, he was not the man to endanger her life and his own… [9]

8 Song written and composed by Felix McGlennan. Words and music reproduced on pages 46 and 47.
9 Quoted from *Grace Darling: Her True Story* by Thomasin Darling and D. Atkinson

Mr Darling's explanation of the rescue in a letter to Trinity House gives us the plain facts:

We agreed that if we could get to them, some of them would be able to assist us back, without which we could not return. [10]

Mr Darling was also doubtful that the lifeboat stationed at Seahouses would put to sea, as he also explained in his letter to Trinity House. Therefore his decision to attempt a rescue was based on sound judgement and a cool calculation that they had a good chance of succeeding.

An oil painting of the wreck by JW Carmichael c.1845

10 Letter dated 6 October, 1838

The Rescue

Constance Smedley claims in her book, *Grace Darling and Her Times,* that the only preparation Grace made for her voyage into history was taking off the petticoats she wore under her green and cream striped dress, which would have dragged heavily as they became soaked with water. There are still remnants of the dress in the museum but they are little more than rags. Grace presented all the garments she wore during the rescue to a Miss Norraby, the granddaughter of the artist Henry Perlee Parker, who painted Grace and came to know her well after the rescue. According to Constance Smedley, snippets of these clothes have been found all over the world.

A framed piece of Grace's dress

Grace's hair was still in its curling rags as she pushed it inside her old straw bonnet. She wrapped a tartan shawl across her chest and tied it behind her back. It wasn't the ideal outfit for an emergency rescue but waterproof coats had not been invented at the time.

Both Thomasin Darling and Constance Smedley claim in their books that Mrs Darling begged her husband and daughter not to go, scolding Grace that if anything happened to Mr Darling, she would never forgive her. However, both authors go on to assert that Mrs Darling relented and did in fact help the rescuers to launch the coble.

The popular belief is that Grace went out alone. Why did this belief arise? It was probably a combination of several things. Following the incident, early newspaper reports stated that Grace carried out the rescue single-handedly. In the excitement which centred around Grace's heroic part in the affair, Mr Darling's role could have been forgotten. To add to the confusion, the coble used in the rescue was called *Grace Darling*. When the story was retold, as it was time and time again, reference to Grace Darling could have meant the young woman or the boat. However, there is also the fact that people write what makes exciting news: Mr Darling's part in the rescue could have been purposefully ignored in order to focus solely on the courageous Grace. Romanticised paintings done at the time of the event also showed Grace alone in the boat, as did the commemorative mugs and china statues that flooded the market. All these helped to cloud the facts and perpetuate the myth.

A painting of Grace, seemingly alone in the coble

Once the coble was launched, Grace took a single light oar while Mr Darling rowed with two much heavier ones. Although the Harcars are less than one kilometre away from Longstone, the rough seas and the tide meant that Mr Darling and Grace had to row twice that distance to avoid being themselves washed onto the rocks. The return journey would be against the wind and tide and would only be possible if some of the survivors were fit enough to help them row. Although the tide had fallen, because of the time of year, a second high tide was due – the Harcars would soon be under water. Time was running out and the survivors were again in imminent danger of drowning.

At high tide it would be almost impossible to land on Big Harcar. However, as the tide fell, a narrow inlet was exposed on the south side of the rock, sheltered from the worst of the northerly winds. At low tide, the sides of the creek rose about three metres out of the water and the rock face was broken in places by small outcrops, jutting out to form natural, irregular steps; these would make a landing on Big Harcar possible, although still very difficult. It was towards this creek that Grace and her father rowed.

As they came alongside Big Harcar, the Darlings' boat was driven towards the rocks and Grace and her father were in danger of being thrown against them. Only a few hundred metres away loomed the hulk of the *Forfarshire*, being battered by the waves that raged on the exposed north side of the reef. The Darlings managed to row into the creek, which was only a little wider than their boat, to where the sea was less turbulent. It was only then that they were able accurately to count the number of people on Big Harcar. There were twelve in all, too many for the coble to hold. Somehow Mr Darling had to get onto the rocks to decide who should be taken off first. Taking the boat as close in as possible, Grace held it steady while her father leapt across the gap onto Big Harcar. Grace, now alone in a boat that normally needed three people at the oars, somehow found the strength and determination to row back and forth through the swell,

The site of the rescue on Big Harcar, shown here at low tide

in an effort to keep the boat away from a disastrous collision. (Constance Smedley writes that, as an old man, Mr. Darling said that leaving Grace alone was, for him, the worst part of the whole event. It may also have contributed to the story that Grace was by herself throughout.)

On the storm-swept rock above, Mr Darling had discovered that three of the people were already dead. Injury and exposure to the atrocious conditions had taken the lives of a middle-aged minister, the Rev. Robb, along with two young children whose mother, a Mrs Dawson, was pitifully cradling their bodies. Mr Darling made the difficult decision to take the woman and leave her dead children behind on Big Harcar. He also chose an injured crew member and three able-bodied sailors for the first trip back to Longstone. Thankfully, his calculated risk paid off, for the sailors were still fit enough to row, two of them taking the oars alongside Mr Darling, while Grace tended the survivors.

Eventually, the party made it back to Longstone where Grace, though exhausted, helped her mother feed, calm and nurse the injured. Meanwhile, Mr Darling and the two sailors set out again for the Harcars to bring back the remaining survivors. Very little other information is known about the survivors, five of whom were from the crew of the *Forfarshire*. Despite undergoing the trauma of shipwreck, and witnessing fear, injury and death, some of the men went out into the storm a second time to bring their fellow survivors back to safety. It is interesting that so little is written about their heroism, and it is Grace's part in the rescue that remains the focus of attention.

By nine o'clock, all nine survivors had been rescued and were safe in the warm kitchen of the Longstone Lighthouse. Mrs Dawson stayed in Grace's bedroom, the injured men were given the boys' bunk beds and the others rested on makeshift beds in the kitchen.

So ended the famous incident. Mr Darling's own account of the rescue in his journal is his usual brief summary and he doesn't mention that Grace was with him. It wasn't until Trinity House requested a fuller account of the matter that he wrote a letter to them explaining her involvement.

How did Grace herself feel about the rescue? Did she have time to stop and think of her own danger? A letter to an unnamed friend gives some idea of her intentions:

> *I had little thought of anything but to exert myself to the utmost, my spirit was worked by the sight of such a dreadful affair that I can imagine I can still see the sea flying over the vessel.* [11]

11 Letter quoted in *Grace Darling and her Time*, by Constance Smedley

It would appear that, under pressure, she had no time to think and there was no room for fear or concern about her own safety. She would have had no idea that she had just rowed her way into the history books.

Northumberland is steeped in legend. There are countless ghosts and sinister hooded monks who walk on the sea and the county has more than its fair share of mysteries. It would therefore seem likely that the locals would have been glad to add the adventure of a local young woman to the list. They could have spiced up the story and profited from the unexpected fame that Grace had brought them. Interestingly, they did just the opposite. While the Victorian media were busy adapting the story, and portrait painters were romanticising Grace's image, the locals did not enter into the fuss over Grace. Indeed, they did the opposite. Some said that the storm wasn't really so bad, or claimed that the survivors saved themselves and walked over the rocks at low tide. Others shrugged off the rescue as something that any of them could have done.

When a local travel writer, William Howitt, visited Longstone in 1840, he found resentment among some of the locals:

The most characteristic thing is, that all the common people about, and particularly the sailors and fishermen, deny her all merit... [12]

Even the harbourmaster at Seahouses claimed:

It's all humbug... They pretend to say that Grace and her father saved the nine people from the wreck; they did nothing of the sort; the people saved themselves. They walked across from the vessel at low water to the next island and the Darlings fetched them off when the water was smooth... [13]

However, Grace's courage had given the Victorian public just what they wanted. She was young, brave, modest and unselfish. Like it or not, the locals had a national hero on their hands.

12 Quoted from *Visits to Remarkable Places*, 1842, by William Howitt
13 Quoted from *Visits to Remarkable Places*, 1842, by William Howitt

Darling Grace!

Grace's courageous deed was by no means the end of the affair, for there had been another attempt to get to the *Forfarshire* that morning and, once again, a Darling was involved. Both *The Journal of William Darling* and *Grace Darling and her Times* confirm that there was another, much less publicised, rescue attempt.

At about the same time that Mr Darling and Grace were setting out towards Big Harcar, a coble was also being launched at Seahouses. The wreck had been sighted from Bamburgh Castle and the cannon fired as a signal. At seven o'clock that morning the news reached Seahouses, which itself was awash because of the storm. The local fishermen, amongst whom were the lifeboat crew, were already on the quay fighting to prevent their possessions from being swept away. The strange twist in this story is that William Brooks Darling, Grace's brother, was helping his friends at Seahouses.

Because the lifeboat was too shallow to launch in such seas, the crew decided to attempt a rescue in one of the fishing cobles. William Brooks, having taken part in many rescues with his father and brothers, joined them. For the next two and a half hours, William Brooks, three brothers William, James and Michael Robson, Thomas Cuthbertson, Robert Knox and William Swan battled through the turbulent seas until they eventually reached the battered wreck. Of course, what they didn't know was that Grace and Mr Darling had got there before them. The exhausted men had no reward for their bravery, for they found only the dead on Big Harcar. The weary and demoralised crew decided that they would never make it back to Seahouses and so made for the Longstone Lighthouse and safety.

The storm continued to rage for another two days and conditions on Longstone were appalling. Because of the number of survivors, there was no room for William Brooks and his friends, who had to sleep in the half-ruined barracks which were flooded at each high tide. Food was running out and the constant task of tending the wounded,

A woodcut of the survivors being cared for in the kitchen of the Longstone

washing bed linen and clothes, cooking and ceaselessly heating water was taking its toll on Grace and her mother. Needless to say, the normal lighthouse duties also had to be carried out. On the third day, the storm abated and the lifeboat crew returned to the mainland.

With them went the news of Grace's rescue of the shipwrecked, and so began her meteoric rise to fame – a fame for which she had no desire.

At first it was the inquests, or legal inquiries, into the deaths of the crew and passengers of the *Forfarshire* that caught the public's attention. There were in fact two inquests. The first seems to have been badly conducted and certain important witnesses weren't called. Based largely on the evidence of one of the survivors, a man called Daniel Donovan, the jury found that the leaking boilers had caused the tragedy and the responsibility of the disaster was placed on the shoulders of the drowned Captain Humble. However, Donovan's evidence was suspect. He had once been a fireman on the *Forfarshire* and it appears that he had been sacked. This raised the question of whether he had a grudge against the shipping line and the captain. If he had, was his evidence reliable? When a few days later, more bodies were washed up on the coast, another inquest was held and the new jury overturned the verdict. Captain Humble's name was cleared and the final verdict was that the wrecking of the *Forfarshire* was caused by tempestuous seas. The disaster had brought the importance of safety at sea and the need for more lifeboats to the attention of the public. Even so, the public interest in the disaster could have waned had it not been for the fact that a young woman was central to the rescue.

The edition of the local newspaper in which Grace's story was first reported

The newspapers turned their attention to Grace. The main fascination was that the hero of the *Forfarshire* incident was a young woman rather than a man. Two local papers reported the story first and sent reporters out to Longstone. They described her thus:

> *But Grace is nothing masculine in her appearance although she has so stout a heart. In person she is about the middle size, of a comely countenance – rather fair for an islander – and with an expression of benevolence and softness most truly feminine in every point of view...* [14]

The reporters from the local papers also seemed surprised by her shyness:

> *When we spoke of her noble and heroic conduct she slightly blushed and appeared anxious to avoid the notice to which it exposed her; she smiled at our praise but said nothing in reply...*

Grace Darling's slipper

The national newspapers were also vigorous in their praise. *The Times* wrote:

> *It is impossible to speak in adequate terms of the unparalleled bravery and disinterestedness shown by Mr Darling and his truly heroic daughter, especially so with regard to the latter... Is there in the whole field of history, or of fiction even, one instance of female heroism to compare for one moment with this?* [15]

Judging by modern standards Grace was quite small. Her dresses in the museum in Bamburgh show that she was about 1m 60cm tall and was slight in build and her slippers show that she had small feet.

---

14 Quoted from a joint article published in the *Berwick and Kelso Warder*, 22 September, 1838 and the *Sunderland Herald*, 23 November, 1838
15 The Times 9 September, 1838

From then on Grace was flooded with letters requesting autographs and locks of hair. Apparently, at the height of her fame, masses of locks of different coloured hair flooded the market, all claiming to be genuine.

Trips to the Farnes were arranged and boatloads of sightseers landed on Longstone. The lighthouse was often invaded by intrusive visitors.

An extract from Grace's journal detailing to whom she sent locks of her hair

A lock of Grace's hair

The modest and reserved Grace found the situation confusing. To some extent she was delighted by people's kindness, but she was also embarrassed by all the attention. William Howitt, who visited the Darling's, noticed that Grace:

shuns public notice, and is even troubled at the visits of the curious.[16]

16 *Visits to Remarkable Places*, 1842

A succession of portrait painters stayed at the Longstone and painted not only Grace, but her mother and father too. Each artist painted her differently from the one before, so we have no real idea of exactly how she looked. The Darlings soon tired of the publicity and Mr Darling put a stop to the artists' visits. Poets, one of whom was William Wordsworth, wrote long and emotional verses, which were often badly written, in praise of Grace's beauty and courage:

> *Pious and pure, modest and yet so brave,*
> *Though young so wise, though meek so resolute –*
> *Might carry to the clouds and to the stars,*
> *Yea, to celestial Choirs, GRACE DARLING'S name!* [17]

A couple of novels were written, based very loosely on her rescue mission. They represented the type of book that Mr Darling disliked so much, because they told the story in an over-dramatic way. One of them took great liberties with Grace's real story and added romance in the form of various young men with names such as St Clair and Fitzroy. The author sent her a copy, enclosing a letter explaining his reasons:

> *On a perusal of its pages you will find there are various scenes and characters of an imaginary nature introduced… and that fiction is frequently mingled with the gravest truths for the purpose of adorning a moral and giving point to a tale.* [18]

Grace replied in her kind way that she wished the author "every success".

Offers of marriage began to arrive in the post, none of which Grace took seriously. However, had she decided to marry, it would seem that she would not have changed her surname, for her sister Thomasin claims that Grace had said that the name Darling:

> *had become a name for sons to be proud of, known throughout the kingdom and beyond.* [19]

17 *Grace Darling* by William Wordsworth. Composed 1842, published 1845
18 Quoted from *Grace Darling, or The Maid of the Isles* by Jerrold Vernon
19 Quoted from *Grace Darling: Her True Story* by Thomasin Darling and D. Atkinson

A portrait of Grace painted in 1838, by Henry Perlee Parker

One of the pottery mugs that appeared on the market in commemoration of the rescue

Grace received many strange offers, but none quite so bizarre as that from a theatre in London asking her to pose in a rowing boat on stage, while a play was acted around her. Not surprisingly, she refused. Grace was showered with unwanted money and gifts and even had a hat named after her.

She also received an enormous amount of fan mail, some of it genuine and some patronising and insincere:

We fancy you so used to the waves that you have pleasure in riding out in a rough sea. [20]

To which Grace replied rather irritably:

A special edition Grace Darling chocolate box

You requested me to let you know whether I felt pleasure to be out in a rough sea, which I can assure you there is none, I think, to any person in their sober senses. [21]

The Duke of Northumberland took great interest in the Darling family and invited both father and daughter to Alnwick Castle, where he presented them with Royal Humane Society Gold Medals. The Duchess gave Grace a letter from Queen Victoria commending her on her bravery and instructing that she should be given the sum of £50. The Northumberlands obviously took a great liking to the young woman and the Duke announced that he wished to treat Grace as his ward. This meant that he became her guardian and was legally responsible for her financial welfare. Considering that the two families were from the opposite ends of society, their relationship was most unusual. However, no matter how great a respect they had for each other, the barriers between the classes had to be recognised. The Darlings were therefore served tea in the servant's quarters! At Christmas the Duke sent a marvellous assortment of presents to Longstone for the family. Amongst these were the first of the new waterproof jackets made by Charles Macintosh, a silver teapot for Mrs Darling and a watch for Grace.

20 Letter, date unknown, sent by Miss S Price of Nottingham
21 Letter dated 25 January, 1839

The Duke continued to take a keen interest in Grace and personally arranged her Trust Fund of £700, a fortune at the time. When he wrote to her asking if she wanted to withdraw any cash, Grace replied that £5 every six months would be all she needed. Fame had not turned her head.

Grace's brother, George, urged her to make the most of her good fortune and strongly disagreed with her reluctance to take advantage of her situation. In 1873, long after Grace's death, George sold the coble to the wealthy Colonel John Joicey. For years it lay rotting on his ornamental lake until, in 1913, Lady John Joicey-Cecil presented it to the Royal National Lifeboat Institution for restoration. George also sold the oar that Grace used in the rescue for £20.

Myth surrounds even the circumstances of Grace's death. A popular belief is that she caught a chill during the rescue; others said that she was worn down by the constant pressures of public attention. Although understandable, there is no real evidence to prove this. Grace actually became unwell nearly four years after the rescue, in the spring of 1842, during a visit to the mainland. At first it seemed to be merely a cold, but when her condition didn't improve, she was sent to stay with her sister, Thomasin, in Bamburgh. Grace had tuberculosis. In the dim cottage, away from the elements of sea, wind and sky which were so natural to her, she lay in a box bed with its sliding doors tightly closed to keep out the air. Here she wrote the last of her many letters:

Dear Father and Mother,

As I canot wright [cannot write] you a long letter this time please God in a little time I will wright [write] a long one.

I am your loving daughter,

Grace H. Darling [22]

22 Letter dated 3 October, 1842.

Grace never wrote that long letter, for Thomasin tells us in her book that she "went like snow" and on 20 October, 1842, Grace died in her father's arms. She was twenty-six years old. Thomasin recounts that Mr Darling "deeply felt the loss" and there is an interval of three months before he takes up his journal again, thought to be as a result of his grief.

Grace's memorial in St Aidan's churchyard, Bamburgh

Conclusion

How should we view Grace Darling today? What is it about her that still fascinates the public? After all, she was a shy, rather unremarkable young woman until those few short hours of heroism elevated her from obscurity to fame. Her life was one of contradictions. Despite her lack of formal education she was surprisingly well-informed and articulate. Her lonely existence could have made her withdrawn, yet she was lively and enjoyed company. Her raw surroundings and the drudgery of the never-ending lighthouse duties could well have roughened her, but she was orderly and refined. It is as though all her past experiences had prepared her for this one great act of courage, but in no way had she been prepared for what followed.

Newspapers still report the story of Grace Darling inaccurately. On 24 March, 1970, the *Sunderland Echo* wrote that Grace and Mr Darling rowed out from St Mary's lighthouse, which is in fact at Whitley Bay, over forty miles south of Longstone.

Even today, while acknowledging Grace's courage, some local people feel that there has never been enough recognition of the bravery of the crew of the Seahouses lifeboat. The claims and counterclaims continue.

In 1993 a national daily newspaper published an article which questioned the severity of the storm during the Darling's rescue of the *Forfarshire* survivors. A north-east meteorologist had researched weather conditions at the time of the rescue and claimed that the reports of the tempestuous seas she faced were greatly exaggerated. He claims:

Few legends of recent times are as embroidered as that of Grace Darling. [23]

The article goes on with a Northumberland tourism officer jumping to Grace's defence:

I don't imagine this weatherman would like to repeat her act. Anyone who goes out into a storm-tossed North Sea in a rowing boat has to be pretty plucky.

Then, into the fray comes a spokesman for the Grace Darling Museum claiming that the meteorologist:

…is talking rubbish. Our researches show the storm was so bad even the Seahouses lifeboat was unable to get there.

In the travel section of another national newspaper, the correspondent visited Bamburgh in 1994 and retold Grace's story. The end of his article echoed the sentimentality of those first newspaper reports and questioned once again the background to her untimely death:

As I stood beside her grave in Bamburgh churchyard, one uncomfortable thought nagged. Was the true killer of this frail, innocent and brave young woman simply TB, (tuberculosis) or was there something behind that: a debility from pressures imposed by a popular acclaim she did not want and could not tolerate? [24]

So, it comes full circle. Sentimentality surfaces again and, despite all the artefacts in the Grace Darling Museum, all the written evidence in William Darling's journal, in letters and in Grace's own correspondence, there are still questions which remain unanswered. Grace Darling remains an enigma.

23 *Daily Mail*, 9 September, 1993
24 *The Daily Telegraph*, 25 June, 1994

Grace Darling Song

Written and composed by
Felix McGlennan

'Twas on the Longstone lighthouse,
There dwelt an English maid:
Pure as the air around her,
Of danger ne'er afraid.
One morning just at daybreak,
A storm toss'd wreck she spied;
And tho' to try seemed madness,
'I'll save the crew!' she cried.

CHORUS

And she pull'd away, o'er the rolling seas,
Over the waters blue.
'Help! Help!' she could hear the cry of
the shipwreck'd crew.
But Grace had an English heart,
And the raging storm she brav'd;
She pull'd away, mid the dashing spray,
And the crew she saved.

They to the rock were clinging,
A crew of nine all told;
Between them and the lighthouse,
The sea like mountains rolled.
Said Grace: 'Come help me, Father,
We'll launch that boat,' said she.
Her father cried: 'Tis madness,
To face that raging sea!'

CHORUS

One murmer'd prayer 'Heav'n guard us!'
And then they were afloat;
Between them and destruction,
The planks of that frail boat.
Then spoke the maiden's father:
'Return or doom'd are we.'
But up spoke brave Grace Darling:
'Alone I'll brave the sea!'

CHORUS

They bravely rode the billows,
And reached the rock at length:
They saved the storm toss'd sailors,
In Heaven alone their strength.
Go, tell the wide world over,
What English pluck can do;
And sing of brave Grace Darling,
Who nobly saved the crew.

CHORUS

'Twas on the Long-stone light-house, There dwelt an Eng-lish maid: Pure

as the air a - round her, Of dan - ger ne'er a - fraid. One

morn - ing just at day-break, A storm-toss'd wreck she spied; And

rit.

tho' to try seemed mad - ness, 'I'll save the crew!' she cried.

Chorus

Tempo di Valse

And she pull'd a - way, o'er the rol - ling seas, O - ver the wa - ters blue.___

'Help! Help!' she could hear the cry of the ship - wreck'd crew.___ But

Grace had an Eng - lish heart,___ And the ra - ging storm she brav'd;___ She

pull'd a - way, mid the dash - ing spray, And the crew she saved.___

Bibliography:

Cresswell, Helen, *The Story of Grace Darling*, Viking Kestrel 1988

Darling, Thomasin and Atkinson, Daniel , *Grace Darling: Her True Story*, 1880

Darling, Thomasin (editor), *The Journal of William Darling 1795-1860*, Hamilton, Adams, and Co. 1886

Mitford, Jessica, *Grace Had an English Heart* Viking 1988

Montgomery, W. A., and Weightman, M. Scott, *The Grace Darling Guidebook*, M.S.Weightman 1974

Pearson, Lynn F., *Lighthouses*, Shire Publications Ltd. 1995

Smedley, Constance, *Grace Darling and her Time*, Mayflower Press 1932

Smedley, Constance, *Grace Darling and Her Islands*, The Religious Tract Society 1933

Garnett, Oliver, *Souter Lighthouse and The Leas*, The National Trust 1995

Index: